WHERE THE WORDS END
AND MY BODY BEGINS

WHERE THE WORDS END
AND MY BODY BEGINS

AMBER DAWN

ARSENAL PULP PRESS ● VANCOUVER

THIRD PRINTING: 2020

ARSENAL PULP PRESS
Suite 202–211 East Georgia St.
Vancouver, BC V6A 1Z6
Canada
arsenalpulp.com

The publisher gratefully acknowledges the support of the Canada Council for the Arts and the British Columbia Arts Council for its publishing program, and the Government of Canada (through the Canada Book Fund) and the Government of British Columbia (through the Book Publishing Tax Credit Program) for its publishing activities.

"Chicken Dance," "Together Six," "Whole Messy Thing," and "On and Up" were previously published in *Adrienne*, Issue 4 (October 2014).

Cover illustration: "Lady of the Pink Lake" by Rebecca Chaperon
Book design by Gerilee McBride
Back cover photo by Bell Ancell

Printed and bound in Canada

Library and Archives Canada Cataloguing in Publication:

Dawn, Amber, 1974–, author
Where the words end and my body begins / Amber Dawn.

Poems.
Issued in print and electronic formats.
ISBN 978-1-55152-583-9 (pbk.).—ISBN 978-1-55152-584-6 (epub)

I. Title.

PS8607.A9598W54 2015   C811'.6   C2015-900399-7
                                                C2015-900400-4

CONTENTS

Acknowledgments & Gratitude

Gratitude to the Musqueam, Squamish, and Tsleil-Waututh Peoples, on whose territory I live and write. Poetry, not pipelines

Thank you:

to all the poets I've glossed and drawn strength from

to the outstanding family at Arsenal Pulp Press

to Rebecca Chaperon for the dreamy cover art

to my Friday morning poetry students, 2013/2014, who I am certain taught me more than I taught them

and to Zena Sharman, Sharon Pink, Giselle da Silva, Eli Manning, Rachel Rees, Ivan Coyote, Billeh Nickerson, Mary Bryson, Janice Stewart, Cement H. Goldberg, Lisa Jean Helps, Jen Sung, Tiare Lani Kela Jung, Alex Leslie, Nomy Lamm, Matthew Walsh, Anna Swanson, and Vivek Shraya

Dedicated to my wife, CJ Rowe, a poet masquerading as an academic

Introduction: GLOSSY SOLIDARITY

The first book of poetry I purchased was P.K. Page's *Hologram: A Book of Glosas* (Brick Books, 1994). I was an arts undergrad, and Page's glosas were a hot topic in the halls of the Creative Writing Program at the University of British Columbia.

The slender volume looked magnificent on my milk-crate bookshelves between a grimy paperback copy of Katherine Dunn's *Geek Love* and some well-handled *Love and Rockets* comics. Once there was a bed bug scare in the building I lived in on East Hastings Street in Vancouver, and P.K. Page's glosas had to be stored in a zip-lock bag in my freezer for safekeeping.

The fourteen glosa poems found in *Hologram* are written with a lyrical sensibility I'll call consanguineous: connected by blood. Indeed, Page has offered us a lineage, a bloodline of language and memory and feeling. I've read *Hologram* again and again (even when the pages were chilly).

I too wanted to gloss. I may never possess the technical mastery Page employed to gloss the works of Rainer Maria Rilke and Elizabeth Bishop. In addition to the strict form—four ten-line stanzas, with the last line of each stanza derived sequentially from a quatrain of another poet—a glosa is an opportunity for a keen poet to interact with their peers and influences. As a young writer, I barely managed feed myself on a good day, much less interact with a poet like Rilke. Nonetheless, I wanted to join the kindred conversation the glosa seemed to facilitate. And so my attempts to gloss began with a search for poets who spoke to me, who seemed to invite me in. I discovered Lucille Clifton, who wrote, "...come celebrate / with me that everyday / something has tried to kill me/and has failed." Yes! I connect with survivorship verse. I want to offer something back to Lucille Clifton.

I found Adrienne Rich's love poems: "We want to live like trees, / sycamores blazing through the sulfuric air, / dappled with scars, still exuberantly budding." Oh, yes please! I understand sharing pain and promise with a lover, with an entire community of lovers, in fact. In Rich's honour, I would create echoing verse.

I spent years seeking poets and verse before I had gathered a long list of quatrain-length quotes. I then approached each chosen quatrain as a writing prompt. This became my daily writing practice, perhaps the most joyful, uncritical work of my creative life. I wasn't bound to narrative (though my poems can be called narrative), and there was no need to concern myself with continuity or plot. As a writer who has worked mainly in prose, this process truly was sanguine: spirited, unhesitating, and "of blood." I even let myself stray from the strict glosa form when breaking the rules served me. Glossing allowed me to immerse myself in a kind of living appreciation for poetry and for the personal memories and values that shape my writing.

All the poets whom I've glossed in this collection find themselves somewhere along the queer, gender-creative, feminist, and/or survivor spectrum. In other words, I've selected a handsome sampling of remarkable voices. These poets are among those who remind me that our tenacity and circumspection has led us to know the world and the word in unique ways. We are not an easy-answers bunch. We are a far cry from the reductive buzz of the dominant narrative. Our work often resists or disrupts just such dominant discourse. We were made to be poets. And I am bound to these and many other poets in an allied exchange of language and significance and possibility. I set out to gloss, and the glosa has offered me a poetic form that embodies the communities and spaces I've always yearned for and revered.

If ever I feel lost, I will gloss.

WHOLE MESSY THING

This sadness is bigger than B vitamins, it
is not interested in working around my schedule, or
all your good ideas, it arrives anyway
on wings of fog and stays awhile

"Love Is a Messy Broken Thing, Part 6," Jacks McNamara

Depression, the word, is useless. There's no music
no romance, no reclaiming it. Neither word nor illness
can be made into bedroom play. Comedy, maybe?
"So a guy walks into a bar ... I mean the ER,
no I mean a bar ... no I mean ER." Same difference.
Divorced from the root
depression divvies, clinically scores me
into that and this and this and this.
But sadness is bigger than my last relapse.
This sadness is bigger than B vitamins, it

is bigger than the SAD lamp that brightens my desk.
Bigger than ten milligrams twice a day.
Sadness holds more than all the second-
hand coffee mugs at an AL-ANON meeting
takes more time than the self-help
workbook my poetics professor gifted me
longer than the long-distance collect call
my mother refused to accept.
Too urgent to be wait-listed, it
is not interested in working around a schedule, or

another referral from the Red Book.
So tremendous, sadness
doesn't know where the world ends
and my body begins.
Sure, no bullshit about communing with the universe
but you won't catch me being laissez-faire
about upper case "W" Wholeness.
I practice sadness because it subsumes
all my shady moods and
all my good ideas. It arrives any way

it can and yet it is always here
like a lake forever fed by a cold creek.
Damn right a nature metaphor!
Want more? Sadness always has more
to offer. Its occupation is fluid. It's air.
Notice you're breathing? Sadness
is as wide as rain on one end of town
and a heaven-sent break in the clouds
on the other and on the other
wings of fog, and all of it stays awhile.

AUTOPHOBIA

Where does one
live when one fits nowhere but in fiction
and insanity? Even today
That's what we call our in-betweens: insane.

"Postulation on the Violent Works of the Marquis de Sade," Elizabeth Bachinsky

At the twenty-bed
psychiatric facility for short-term
crisis intervention I was
given my own room, the intake
nurse told me I was lucky
that so few women
were checked-in.
Men hemmed the common room.
The biggest always wore his fly undone.
Where does one

.

heal when the wound
is diagnosed a disorder?
Each morning at ten I joined the other
patients in mandatory art therapy.
I obliged yarn and popsicle sticks. The therapist
asked, "What have you made, Amber Dawn?"
I said, "A bird house
where no bird will never nest."
Where else can the absent
live when one fits nowhere but in fiction?

Only the spine-broken
Grimm's Fairy Tales shelved in the quiet room
offered reason, babe in the woods
juniper tree. When the therapist put pens
in our hands and bid us to "personify
our feelings" I tantrumed, scared
to write my own name
at the top corner of the page.
Autophobia: to fear oneself. Loathing
and insanity. Even today

I sometimes crave that Haldol injection
long sleep, then scores of slurred speech
I voluntarily discharged the day
we were supposed to draw a body map.
I was angry, lying on the butcher's
paper. My empty silhouette profane.
Coloured crayons and glitter glue ragged.
I told the intake nurse I no longer heard voices.
She said, "Treatment's not for nits and crybabies."
That's what we call our in-betweens. Insane!

MOTHER DID HER OWN STUNTS

Still no body wants to become no body.
Remember that when you are discovered
in all your figura
borders of the Real, surrounded

"notes toward dropping out," Trish Salah

Film stock: 16 mm Kodascope magenta
cyan and yellow slipped into fata morgana
in this thermal decade you eat yogurt and honey.
Location: 244 Prospect Point Road South
Algae-fouled headline "Lake Erie Is Dead!"
Your backyard realism. Genre: biography
Cinematography: subjective shot from your child
's POV. The audience sees what you see
or should the subject act candid, like cinéma vérité?
Still no body wants to become no body

a long shot, perhaps, a comfortable distance
from the camera? Mise-en-scène: optimistic poor décor
imagine a thousand eager eyes in the knotty pine panels
an avocado green refrigerator supports domestic equilibrium.
When does set dressing possess enough personality
to become character? Low-key lighting: shadow-smothered
June afternoon. Diegetic sound: door slam
woman scream, backhand. (You can do this, pretend
it's a movie. Snap the black clapperboard.
Remember that when you are discovered

to say you weren't in it for acclaim, just truth.)
Props: a daisy print vinyl highchair
Minnie Mouse spoon. Your mother
and father enter the frame, moving
characters, landed migrants,
theirs was a deserter era. Broken dreamers.
Dialogue: Don't you dare hit me
in front of my child. (Do it
use ciné to interpret injury.)
In all your figura

etymologica can this be resolved? The illusion
is ludicrous, the picture painted to your hindsight
's specifications: catsup red. Prop: 38-ounce glass bottle
of Heinz. Your mother's close-up, her breakneck swing.
The foley uses the sound of a supernova
a collapsed star. Brilliant! Costume: blood
and tomato, glass shard crown. What if
your father never got up from the ground?
Letterbox what memory has recorded
borders of the Real, surrounded

CHICKEN DANCE

CHICKEN
Pheasant and chicken, chicken is a peculiar third.
CHICKEN
Alas a dirty word, alas a dirty third alas a dirty third, alas a dirty bird

    "Tender Buttons (Chicken)," Gertrude Stein

"C" that's the way it begins
in high school I had really great tits, naturally
the guidance counselor foresaw strip tease
please pleasing pleasure dome home-o "H"
that's the next letter in, alas jobless working-class
in truth my high school was too down-turn bitten
to employ a guidance counselor "I" in the middle
of the word, no cheerleading coach either, our squad
shook grab-ass, our reputation was over-ridden
CHICKEN

our after-school program was Alcoholics Anonymous
alas, empty shot glass, addicts adding up arrivederci
our school motto DI NATUS SQUALUS
PER MORTEM SQUALUS
(Latin: Born a Dirtbag, Die a Dirtbag)
dirty pillow dirty hair not rare but game birds
"C" you've already heard the one about
bittersweet sixteen, the bumfuck ballet
around the brass pole a dollar bill a credit card
a pheasant and chicken, chicken is a peculiar third

gender sex
worker straight-for-pay pheasant fluffer
normative hetero-norma-tittie spectacle,
a marquee of really great tits.
"K" now you're rounding the bend
pheasants have slippery heartbroken
laps greased in duck fat or premature
nature nurture torture tutor schooled ass
alas in the woozy air, head in the oven
CHICKEN

it's called a lap dance not a rock-bottom dance
"E" now you're nearing the end
of the night the when the house lights
unmask stretchmark blues, alas a new bruise
alas, stiletto shoes, stabbing dagger
piecing poultry tit-side up on a clean surface
the wishbone is easy to handle
that's the way you spell CHICKEN
and that's how it happened, word for word
Alas a dirty word, alas a dirty third alas a dirty third, alas a dirty bird

VAGINA CANTATA

How we applauded you, pint-sized tart
singing and swinging to *A Cowboy's Sweetheart*.
Who taught you the art of sashay, of rouge,
The French manicure. Who taught you to bruise?

"American Pageant," Rachel Rose

Don't pump the wand inside the tube
like that, it will dry out your mascara.

You've got lipstick on your teeth.
We paint our mouths poppy or pink

so men think of talking vulvas. Vagina cantata:
"Can she bake a cherry pie, Billy Boy, Billy Boy?"

Patent leather, mount up. Tie a ribbon round the oak.
A mix of Giganta and Kewpie is the desired look.

The pubic bone is a predictable body part.
How we applauded you, pint-sized tart.

You're one of us, gobble-gobble, we accept.
Are you ready to rule your nympholepts?

Trust your idiosyncratic gut and follow
these step-by-step instructions.

Don't be nervous, men would rather
buy your used panties than pay child support.

After all they deserve, just deserts, desert ride
the long hot hot long long hot desert ride.

A mirage is mostly water vapor, play your fluid part
singing and swinging to A Cowboy's Sweetheart.

whistling and throb-gristling to Country Comfort.
trilling and shit-uphilling to Old Red Dirt.

"She can bake a cherry pie, quick as a cat can wink her eye
She's a young thing, and cannot leave her mother."

Loneliness is cured on the cactus farm. Nostalgia
likes his feet scrubbed clean by the muse.

Never put the money in your purse, darling fool
gold suede Gucci is a decoy, a fake for the taking.

Risky business, what was your first clue?
Who taught you the art of sashay, of rouge?

Who set for you a chair? Put them ringlets in your hair?
Stuck a pearl in your navel? Invited you to our fine table?

"Did she bid you come in, Billy Boy, Billy Boy
Did she bid you to come in, Charming Billy?"

Torch songs warm tongues. Get it now, while you're young.
Who taught you what's good for the gander is good for the goose?

Who said a honda knot rubbed on rock will come loose?
Who taught you how to play a couch quail? Flash that tail.

Hat your rack. How to moonlight coo. Ungate your sluice.
The French manicure. Who taught you to bruise?

STORY BOOK

      come celebrate
with me that everyday
something has tried to kill me
and has failed.

  "won't you celebrate with me," Lucille Clifton

    Be here with me only if you can.
The 1900 block of Pandora
is where I was raped by three men.
    You don't have to do anything but listen.
I followed my blood into mildewed floorboards
and resurfaced with contusions, wounds
and a pelvic injury commonly called "open book"
fracture—sharp farce medical slang.
My episodic memory has tried to blank the page
and has failed

thanks to the influx
of queers who gentrified Pandora. Many years later
I find myself dancing to "Knock on Wood" remixed
three doors away. The kiddie stroll pushed
still persevering. I take a breather and there's Viv
in her same scuffed pumps. "Hey girl, you live tonight?"
I tell her I retired. She laughs like she doubts it.
A fifth of corn whiskey wreaks sour vomit,
fever spell, recall. Some butch holds my hair.
Something has tried to kill me

something I'd call a curse
but superstition invites too much distrust
    so let's approach this as story.
Once upon an early childhood, sackcloth and ash
took up my hands, one nicked my lips, the other
horned between my thighs, one pinked my eye
the other marked my voice.
    If possible, hear me tell a different story.
Survivorship is not hard stars, it's not a dim fable fucking
with me. That everyday

it is a blessing to wear this skin, gold thread
the fine cloth of outliving. I return to Pandora.
Today there is a play space three doors away.
Chosen family in leather welcome one another.
I don't easily bruise when I stand
for my wife's single tail. "Tell me just how good
I am," I say. "So good good so good so my love my good."
Good brightens the room, beaming blank page.
New story. New street. Enough new stars to share, may we all
come celebrate.

QUEER INFINITY

I'm angry. I'll take back the night. Using me to
swoon at your questionable light,
you had me chasing you,
the world's worst lover, over and over

   "I'm over the Moon," Brenda Shaughnessy

We tried to make the 00s a hold-fast decade. Many of us
got sober or adopted cockeyed dogs named Radar.
We craved long-term goals, five-year plans, but why
when this time the world really seemed to be ending?
Supermoon. Katrina. Cyclone Stan. Frankenstorm.
Icecaps melted in our ozone epoch, bubbles burst. We knew
there'd be no reply during the Tsunami, still we phoned
Kerala and Chaing Mai. Our queer transmigrant families
span the four corners, there's crisis in every time zone. It's true
I'm angry. I'll take back the night. Use me to

call Amsterdam at midnight to relay a friend's death notice.
Use your car to drive to the airport and to the airport again.
Use her stovetop to make two-weeks' worth of one-pot meals
for the freezer. Use my axe to chop wood for the funeral fire.
Use each other's raw bodies to remind ourselves how to pray.
Queer grief is a blueprint. We got this shit wired tight.
Maybe we've become too good at losing? Are we trauma
bonded? I can't speak for the whole, only myself
I'd sooner howl at a wounded moon, yes, I might
swoon at a questionable light

but at least I still swoon—my scabby kneecaps
may always weep pink, I'm so often floored.
I'll never be a two-feet-on-the-ground girl. Let me guess
age didn't temper your passion either? Your passion, like mine
only became more strategic. It's not called a movement
for nothing! Anonymous or rough, queer sex was our *coup
de coeur.* Many of us couldn't love ourselves
until our gaping pasts were licked like wounds.
Young guns in leather boots, odd ones with knuckle tattoos
you had me chasing you

for years before I understood what I was after—an antidote
that smote with the same sweet fever as the venom. Pain
can be fine if you share the sting, stomach the poison together.
Many of us gathered our lovers, renamed friends sister and brother.
We wrote the books that queerlings now read in college. We made
films to screen at Sundance. Our scrappy manifestos got exposure,
one million YouTube views. Let's erect guerrilla monuments
to those who didn't make it. Never confuse hold fast with hold still.
There's so much yet to do. Swoon. I say swoon forever! Apathy is
the world's worst lover, over and over

Queer Infinity

QUEER GRACE

No one has imagined us. We want to live like trees,
sycamores blazing through the sulfuric air,
dappled with scars, still exuberantly budding,
our animal passion rooted in the city.

   "Twenty-one Love Poems," Adrienne Rich

Quiet, you whippersnappers. You were born in the eighties
and I must school you. Our foremamas and papas
didn't have the luxury of safe assembly, much less
Facebook. Think Stonewall had a hashtag?
Allen Ginsberg just yelled, "Defend the Fairies."
#fuckingriot #dragbomb. Boom, queer speech
had to boom to be heard in real time.
Queer gait was a march. Queer hearth was our rage.
We shared the meager feast or starved. Potluck.
No one imagined us. We wanted to live like trees

or at least weeds. We wanted to take root.
Many of us still sow a humble seed to grow
temporary space, knowing that a single moment can
turn it all to rot. I've been involved with the rise and fall
of a handful of radical underground conclaves.
Only queer kin can show you the way
out of the merciless bright mainstream.
Away from the gentrifying rows
of condos and Starbucks and capital influx. Past
sycamores blazing through the sulfuric air.

Past the tar-patched dead-ended streets
to one thousand square feet of damp concrete
nestled under a union-worker-built bridge. I tell you
it's worth it to find yourself, no matter how briefly
in a community-driven, collectively-run, anti-capitalist
gender nonconforming, sex-positive hotspot.
Here. Now. Raise our voices.
Here. Now. Shake our asses.
Our asses are hairy warriors. Thick hips. Our asses are
dappled with scars, still exuberantly budding

with desire: daisy chain, finger cuffs, fisting the forsaken mystery
right out of each other. Fucking the magic back into our bodies.
This grace is ours. This grace is no holds barred. Believe me
I have lovers and friends from Berlin to Brooklyn, the same radical
spaces exist there, but don't take this grace for granted.
Let me remind you that a few hundred queers gathered
in unlicensed warehouses for orgies or for organizing is still considered
a disruption. Let me remind you queer roots reach deep.
Never forget the graves of our foremamas and papas, like
our animal passion, are rooted underground.

COUNTRY MICE

crickets, monarchs, paints and sparrows
frenchman river, sweet grass sky holds still
out here everything stops
for the wind

   "everything holds still for the wind," Leah Horlick

We find each other
in the cosmopolitan squint, polished
concrete, smoked chrome rooms.
She's hard to peg at first
lace dress chic, prosecco cocktail
starry in her hand. She's been
chin-upped by the west. Tested
by an incomprehensible horizon
and passed, but for her pose and bend.
For the wind

that sweeps the wide-open
motherland has left her
with a slant stance, sideways
as corn bowed to a storm.
I too am made
from orchard and axe, crop
and scythe, harvest born
humble earth miles and years
behind me. It's all rock
out here. Everything stops

making sense in the seam
of mountains and million
dollar condos, high-rise residential
more density, more gravel, more glass, more.
Where I come from elevators
are for nursing homes or sawmills.
She sees the soiled knees of my jeans
knows I kneel to a once-was prayer
late waterways, bygone wells
forgotten river. Sweet grass sky holds still

during these vigils, holds space
for choked swamp, cedar stump
tributaries split from the ocean
Vancouver's bloodstone—step forward.
My home is a backwards stamp, like hers.
parched-lawn green, forever level.
Now we find each other turned by urban obstacles.
The far-removed markers we share and seek
chokecherries, ink caps, chorus frogs, golden yarrow
crickets, monarchs, paints and sparrows

DIRT BAG LOVE AFFAIR

My art will be to meet you on the street,
naked palms pressed together, mouths
open wide with pointed tongues. My instinct
is to bear witness to new winter and cold

"Winter Night," Chandra Mayor

What does a riverbank girl become
when she hasn't heard the early spring scream
of ice breaking in over twenty years?
Only women scream in a city of one million
scream to fend off pain or to remember it.
My talent for spotting bobcat tracks is obsolete
in a city of one million. Sometimes a sallow coyote
passes my back window. Would I still be a poet
if I stayed in the sweep of winter wheat?
My art will be to meet you on the street

before curbside trash is collected or corner stores
roll back their gated doors. While one million sleep
we will prowl feral as our scrub-brush birthplaces.
Sure, I've heard you use "opacity" and "vis-à-vis"
in a sentence, but you are no more civilized than slash
field burning, set the wild running, our inborn vowels
warning warning. Push me onward
bear down. Am I the sick one
in the pack? Run me aground
naked palms pressed together, mouths

drooling with illogic. Spit it out, my tempered graces.
Gag it up, my overthinking. Choke me
mindless or choke me blue. I'm aware I'll die
in a city, so will you. Estranged from back wood
river bed   dead   end. My art will be
to meet you in our humble distant
pasts. Praise our roots with skin and bone.
I want you inside me, deeper than all
the lamentable reasons we left home.
Open me wide with pointed tongues. My instincts

are impaired by metropolitan persona
but you make me remember the dirt
I came from. You make me remember when
every sound heard before dawn was wild.
Let's show this city of one million how wild
music can still be made. My art is to hold
your blue-bred body to mine
like landfast ice hugs the shoreline. Like drift ice
I'll let this frozen river move me. My poem
is to bear witness to new winter and cold

ON AND UP

Does the road wind up-hill all the way?
Yes, to the very end.
Will the day's journey take the whole long day?
From morn to night, my friend.

  "Up-Hill," Christina Rossetti

Coffee, cat piss, wood rot, trash
or is it me?—that smell? Poverty
or dropout bouquet, either way
it scents wherever I can afford to be.
My clit was found in a railway yard.
Is that still how it's done these days?
My tongue loosened around the fire pit
Ashes! Ashes! is what I learned to say.
How many rhymes are made from scarcity?
Does the road wind up-hill all the way?

You can't compare plenty and not
if you have never known plenty.
Money is a poor man's myth.
Keep with grit, throw a ravishing fit
from time to time, yes, the world's unfair
but keep with grit, backbend
with nimble glory. Spare this path
and this poem the burden of have-not want.
Be tough-seasoned
yes, to the very end.

I never thought that I'd see thirty and I have
trouble with the end—the very idea of arriving.
I've had to start over and start again.
Will I be drawn a saltwater bath?
I have scabs and cannot stop picking them.
Will I share a bed or sleep alone?
Will there be young flames to keep me warm?
I have more questions. I wrote them down.
Oh yes, will longing claim its own veracity?
Will the day's journey take the whole long day?

We're already a good ways up.
Just look at the wild tracks behind—deer
bear, little nymph, whatever forms you have taken
not one of your selves will be forsaken.
Go together, push on, push up, by dawn
we'll be sore-footed, but mad for love, rake-shaken
eye-to-eyed, yes, the vistas to behold, yes
tired thighs to unfold, yes, these flashbacks are as good
as gold, but ask how far this landscape extends
From morn to night, my friend, my friend.

QUEER LAND

Which lifetime? Beyond what brawn? Who
Knew where the road would take us?
Neat, neat, the rows of apple trees
There in the valley, red summers, the heat

  "Endless Inter-States," Sina Queyras

Something happened to me at Back Roads Pizza in Santa Fe
New Mexico. Locals say the land is magick although
white people are always claiming land
is magick. The woman who nonconsensually hugged
too long wore bone jewellery worshipped Gaia and wanted me
to know that because I live in this world I must love
all the world. Over her shoulder I watched genderqueer
acrobats valdez on the pool table, a loner empty his flask
into a can of cola. I ached with odd longing, but from
which lifetime? Beyond what brawn? Who

or what was I lovesick for? Crying can
help—eyeball orgasms release endorphins and past lives
psychic saltwater, they say. I licked a ramekin of pepper milk gravy
clean at Ria's Bluebird in Atlanta Georgia. Simone de la Ghetto bent
Clyde over the picnic table, Juba carefully considered huevos
Jerry Lee his bacon, Annie Oakley and Scarlot Harlot's
cardinal manes bookended the morning, the movement, the mantra
we are artists innovators geniuses geniuses innovators artists artists
innovators and we are hungry and infinity. I presumed I
knew where the road would take us

not the Interstate, the intersections of our remarkable survival
would be the place we landed. I was younger and homecoming
seemed far more romantic than fuck-cumming.
Queer fuck was everywhere, home was a blue-sky all but
sci-fi idea. Maybe Fancyland in Humboldt County, California?
Maybe Idyll Dandy near Nashville, Tennessee? A place
with a goat named Ally Sheedy, the free chickens all Kikis.
That's the dream, right? On the other side of mighty America?
Where eggs in the nest aren't normal, normal. Grapevines aren't
neat, neat. The rows of apple trees

aren't really rows at all, just fruit handsomely idling
like the lackadaisical stacks of books at Modern Times Collective
in San Francisco where I abandoned the pages of *Go Magazine*
to scope the daydreamy staff person behind the till. Their name
pronoun(s) relationship status dating preferences and kinks: unknown.
But so precious with the paperback spine of *The Left Hand
of Darkness*, I imagined my daisy print underwear in their teeth.
I carried my fantasies along scorching 24th Street. Why must I
wear black in August? I always fall in flummoxed love
there in the valley, red summers, the heat.

THREE PORTRAITS OF FEMME QUEENS, OUSTED

Oh yes, they said I could be a feminist
That is, of course
As long as I don't ask any questions

"Black Feminist," Jillian Christmas

Jamie Lee Hamilton can drum fire
if she needs to, and she needs to because who else
but a Two Spirit Trans Princess would take up thunder
for thirty years, and counting? Sound the alarm
the war against whores always coming. Brothers
sentenced to AIDS quarantine. Sisters run out of the village.
Kith turned on kin. Rainbow citizens became *real* citizens
and became just as capable of cleansing brothel culture
wiping hustler-blood from the gaybourhood. Who shouldered
67 pairs of stiletto shoes up the sentinel-like steps of City Hall?
One shoe for each missing woman. Who suffered February's
frost as she slept on the civic lawn? "We're disappearing"
Jamie Lee Hamiliton waited for council to hear her.
Who among us was pronounced an "urban tragedy"
by the Supreme Court? Who is disappearing?
As long as we don't ask any questions

our enemies can assume the likeness of allies. State-sanctioned
status remains a widely believed myth. Normativity mimics
victory, not a washing of hands, a goodnight kiss. Trish Kelly
monologued about female masturbation in a one-woman show
in a fringe theatre, in the liberal nineties. Meanwhile, she
pinched pierogi with babas at the Ukrainian Hall. Meanwhile
she danced her tradition—jig, belt, and broom. Meanwhile, she
cared for her dying Métis mother. Meanwhile, she aired
riot grrrl revolution on the radio. When she remembered
the hunger of her childhood, she began the good fight for food
First Nations agriculture, backyard chickens, fair-trade mangos
no to GMO, less footprint, less hunger, justice. She ran for election
and the national news headlined, "Would you vote for a female
politician who spoke openly about masturbation?" Be a woman
candidate, a femme fighter, even a mixed-race, bi-sexual, in between
That is, of course

if your vagina shuts the fuck up. Better yet, if your body has never spoken a word. But what about the bodies that make statements just by being? Jillian Christmas, slam champion, queen bee bard asks if there are any Patti Smith fans in the audience. Mostly white hands rally up, then deflate back down as she reads "In response to Patti Smith's 'Rock N Roll Nigger.'" The menacing N-word from the mouth of a black woman, spoken in a room of white ears another brick kicked out from the dominion's bedrock. Do we cheer as mortar dust rises? Clap our hands? Laugh at the appropriate places as Jillian Christmas performs? Like other outliers, she never signed up for the position of breaking the all-mighty promise—pink and white happiness, sister happiness, old icon happiness cracked by uncomfortable blackness. Jillian Christmas says, "We're all in this together." What are we all in? Feminism? Solidarity? Smashing the what the fuck? "I could be a feminist as long as I don't talk about this black girl body." Jillian Christmas says *"Oh yes. They said I could be a feminist."*

SANDRA ANNA'S BABY BOOK

what the future suggests in its advance
everything so closed, even us
and i am writing to bring you back
to where my eyes meet your skin at the periphery

"to bring you home," Ritz Chow

I am my mother's only (living)
child. Her navel popped during peach
and bush-cricket season. She grew sugar snap
peas and kept penned rabbits. Her root cellar
filled with jam and pickles. "Amber Dawn"
she wrote my name in her Baby Book. She was ready.
I was born not at dawn, but around four in the afternoon
I left her womb quickly. Cap of damp curls.
Ten fingers. Ten toes. Eye colour: too dark to be sure.
What the future suggested in its advance

is that I would grow up sweet
on homemade preserves. Grow up honest
in the eastern woodlands. I have imagined her
nursing me, the newborn with eyes like a black dog's.
Our mismatched irides cued the imparity of our lives.
I fixed my sight on distance, on outrunning
the mean line of drunken men
who molder our family tree. I inherited
detachment. The early age I learned to tender
everything so closed, even us

and-them-ed my own
mother. Lumped her in
with her men and her talent
for keeping quiet. I shaved my head in high school.
At first, with a borrowed electric razor, then cut
to the quick with a disposable Bic. Her second husband
had been coming at me—fists, lips, and dick. My scalp
called out help (unheard). After that, I called louder.
After that, my curls never really grew back.
And I am writing to bring you back

Mamma. I've been working lines and verse
for long enough now to finally find you
in the white space. I've claimed the page
is where a poet heals. So I offer this poem
as our long-ago cricket song, our brightly-lit cellar door
our spray of new maple keys on the forest floor.
You've asked me to forgive, and maybe this is how.
I am ready to look now. See the other side of this dated
boundary, there lies a love between blood-tough women,
to where my eyes meet your skin at the periphery

PIÈCE DE RÉSISTANCE

what makes someone capable
of creating a new paradigm
and living it?
who owns that willingness to create

   "unspoken," Lydia Kwa

Over five-dollar lattes a dear old and I reminisce
upon our all time favourite suicide plans.
"XYZ pharmacy," I say. "Buy shady methadone then head up
Hastings to the Second Empire skyscraper. I have a rooftop key."
"Wonder if you can still score fizzies at XYZ"? dear old asks.
She makes culture for the City now, me University. Square pegs
cobbled into round holes, grey mare whores in a greener graze
do we miss the glory days? Retrospect blur
I can look back until I see double.
What makes one capable

of so much change? (hand-to-mouth survival is off the schedule
and it seems that I freed up time for existential questions.)
Aesthetics fluxed when I realized I'd live.
All that beauty that once wanted nothing
to do with me, is now ubiquitous.
Beau monde pink is my newest mentor. Colour therapy?
Whatever helps us carry on, there are no wrongs.
Forgiveness is tactile learning: touch, movement, sound, repeat.
Self-love mastered by mnemonics, the sing-song rhyme
of creating a new paradigm

we hear with our **ear**, **R**hythm **H**elps
Your **T**ender **H**eart **M**ove and the wise
old O.W.L. lived in an oak, the more she Saw the less she Spoke.
There is a question I still haven't answered in verse
What happened to the others?
I lost more than mercury and sweat
during detox. Where's my down-at-the-heel
line, come-up dreamers, beasties, the pretty brass
those existing by the minute
and living it

so close to the bone? Where's their microphone? What stage
has been erected for the disaffected? What wall to mount
a cracked-jaw collage? The exhibition hall is narrow space.
Think of the minds mislaid in the pinch.
Oh but how loss makes us look for glint and change.
One Empire's trash is our pièce de résistance. Are you like me?
Did you have to see the precise shade of your own spilled blood
before you knew what you must do? Then you also know struggle
and art-making can be the same. Then you also understand
who owns that willingness to create.

A GROUP OF SLUTS IS CALLED WHAT?

What I said I pretty much meant
What I am has multiplied and divided
What I stole has been taken away from me and
What I have stumbled upon has pleased me most

"Going Back," Eli Coppola

Creampie is what I saw at the Kitten Theatre
a clutter of cats a kindle of kittens
a dole of turtles a dule of turtledoves
A what? a "gape" of porn stars is what I saw
This is the most used vowel in the English language
What is "schwa"? / ə/ ə/ ə/ in a French accent
like *dis-le* (say it) A what? a "slap"
of masturbators a "fairytale" of jacks
Looking back this was a blessed event
What I said I pretty much meant

the internet is a boner killer
everyone watches gang bangs from home
and the Kitten Theatre is now a Pottery Barn
Somewhere there are still dykes in ratty blonde wigs
working the brass pole, right? Somewhere a twink
in silver briefs teabags a widower's eyelid?
My desire dates me I wanna go back to the 80s
(but without the cocaine). A what? a "stellar"
of bar stars a "heist" of queer diamonds
What I am has multiplied and divided

into personalities and paragraphs
line-by-line edits: I have an office key
I have a well-behaved Pomeranian
a set of Oneida flatware and yet a bullwhip
made of braided kangaroo hide I crack
off-colour jokes for kids who will never understand
the punch line I sleep tight with 5 mg of Ambien
What I have is imposter syndrome I still have
a proud scar I can still speak with a forked tongue
What I stole has been taken away from me and

a what? a "recall" of memories is what
remains do you remember when we all got bent?
a peep of chickens a clutch of chicks
A what? a "fluff" of aging sluts
A what? a "muff" of ex-lovers
all gathered on the same coast
the same city the same black-lit leather bar
the last homocile standing I'll hold the ceiling up
with my spare hand my creampie is still grandiose
What I have stumbled upon has pleased me most

THE REVERED FEMME BOTTOM

I love every loud mouthed hard assed fuck with you
skin soft like a loquat as they punch your cunt into infinity femme
I love girls who will fuck you up for no
and every good reason

"I Love Hard Girls," Leah Lakshmi Piepzna-Samarashinha

The first woman (besides your mother) to slap your face
painted her bedroom floor red a few days before your date
and your knees sank into gummy coats of enamel while she
made you wait. Her window was wide open, undraped, and August
heat bulldozed in and all your sounds blow-horned out.
She said *relax your jaw* and you wondered what made her choose
leather and if your cheeks smarted as handsome bright
as the floorboards. Afterwards her pupils
were lust-drug dilated. *I love a dirty fuck* she cooed
I love every loud mouthed hard assed fuck. With you

being so spring chicken—you hardly knew
what you loved but you bought yourself
a harness and cock at the womyn's sex shop
and joined the other dykes in the phallus procession.
The dog collar and wrist cuffs acquired for fashion
or foreshadowing. Lip piercings damned your smile.
Your scalp confessed to a Bic razor. You made anger your order.
When you pronounced your cunt a warrior the daddies
trained their mad eyes on you. Suited denim rough, but bare
skin soft like a loquat as they punched your cunt into infinity. Femme

you never considered yourself femme
until a lover hailed you, *femme slut pretty pretty*
Honorific. Femme meant worship
this lover, devoted, *Please, femme-gasm*
for me, soak the sheets with your femme
If memory serves, this may have been
the first time you were proud of your body.
Only a fire-gut can ejaculate like you.
A sparkplug sweet thing. A true
lover of girls who will fuck you up. For no

one could have told you
the dearest souls roll rough trade.
This bit of brilliance showed itself bit by bit.
Fuck by loud-mouthed hard-assed fuck you learned
to receive adoration just as well as you took a beating.
No one could have told you adoration
would trial and thrill you more than welts
on your young skin. Reverence's markings
are permanent, and so reverence you were given
and for every good reason

QUEER AS WIVES

Let the bird escape this time
I ask you is this the beginning. This hunger.
All the petals.
Like roses flowing from autumn to May.

"Lead Blues," Anne-Marie Alonzo

You took up with me and I took
your fisting virginity.
In part, it was a matter of dimension
my runt hand can slip through any knothole.
More so, you were ready
to have your pigeon coop cleaned, to join
our bloodlines. Did you know a dove's blood is forever?
Maybe my fist is more sentimental than rebel?
Let's both admit gut fucking has made us saccharine.
Let the bird escape this time

wing out of our wedding cake. Let old world
traditions belong to us; heather sprig
in my shoe, calla lilies round our mothers' wrists
wine sipped from a turned walnut goblet
We wed on the Salish Sea, adjacent harbour
to the basalt rock bank where we first kissed
for an audience of young seals. We kissed
as newlyweds for a gathering of homo-kin, kink-kind
poly-tribe, elders, new juice, healers everyone.
I ask you is this the beginning? This hunger

that keeps my belly asking. This desire
to bind the knot tighter, still tighter.
I've seen what rope does to your throat.
Your eyes alight with all the stars
in Sagittarius, milk dipper, fire archer.
I know the deluge of our love, all meteor showers
all summer spittle, all red dust rain, all free fall fruit
all aspen seeds, all thunderclap, all fireflies
all sugar sand, all downy feathers
all the petals

from all the blossoming
cherry trees along Cordova Street.
Abundance is what marriage has gifted
an endowment of effect and emotion.
I wear your ring on my right hand
my fisting hand—old world meets tootsie
tradition. We pull from forbears and forthcoming.
Root down deep in the unsifted soil
of one another. Love in our strange bird ways
like roses flowing from autumn to May.

TOGETHER SIX

I watched your breast which was fuller than
the night on my porch when I first undid
your buttons. The sheet beneath you was green
It was almost our anniversary

"Epiphyte 2: Moss," Jane Eaton Hamilton

I watch your breast which is fuller than
when we met   I thought you were starving
rawboned butch   lap like a wooden chair
I vowed to feed you
everything I had   tender a feast
charm your tongue
with salted green peas   drunken apricots
sweet sun tea   gradually
your ribs sank into waxing flesh
I'd come to know like my own

the night on my porch when I first undid
the milkmaid braid from my hair
my temples daubed with rose oil   baby
powered scalp elder cedar crooning
in the yard   early peonies   olfactory romance
June's warm spell   an invitation
to strip down   are undressed bodies always
allegory?   our love made us fabulists
we tell our story   and tell it again
when I tug your shirt sleeve   open

your buttons. The sheet beneath you is green
buffalo plaid   banked by patchwork quilts
this is our December bed
the yarn of our winters
frost hugs the window
we wear gooseflesh   yawning skin
you sing "Frosty le bonhomme"   and my heart
becomes a snow globe   each glittering
snowflake chimes, "I'm yours
I'm yours I'm yours"

it is almost our anniversary
when northern flickers hammer our roof
in the morning   magnolia buds split
their pink lips   I lick
the same raindrop off the tip
of your nose as I've licked
for the last six springs
it still tastes like a vow   but today
I will write a poem
to mark the occasion

POEMS CITED

Alonzo, Anne-Marie. "Lead Blues," *Lead Blues*. Guernica Editions, 1990.

Bachinsky, Elizabeth. "Postulation on the Violent Works of the Marquis de Sade," *Fist of the Spider Woman: Tales of Fear and Queer Desire*. Arsenal Pulp Press, 2009.

Chow, Ritz. "to bring you home," *Swallowing Clouds: An Anthology of Chinese-Canadian Poetry*. Arsenal Pulp Press, 2002.

Christmas, Jillian. "Black Feminist," *Matrix Magazine* 98, 2014.

Clifton, Lucille. "won't you celebrate with me," *Book of Light*. Copper Canyon Press, 1992.

Coppola, Eli. "Going Back," *Some Angels Wear Black*. Manic D Press, 2005.

Hamilton, Jane Eaton. "Epiphyte 2: Moss," *Canadian Women's Studies* 16, no. 2, 1996.

Horlick, Leah. "everything holds still for the wind," *Riot Lung*. Thistledown Press, 2012.

Kwa, Lydia. "unspoken,"*sinuous*. Turnstone Press, 2013.

Mayor, Chandra. "Winter Night," *Post-Prairie: An Anthology of New Poetry*. Talonbooks, 2005.

McNamara, Jacks. "Love Is a Messy, Broken Thing. Part 6," *Inbetweenland*. Deviant Type Press, 2013.

Piepzna-Samarasinha, Leah Lakshmi. "I Love Hard Girls," *PRISM International* 52 no. 2, 2014.

Queyras, Sina. "Endless Inter-States," *Expressway*. Coach House Books, 2009.

Rich, Adrienne. "Twenty-one Love Poems," *The Dream of a Common Language*. W.W. Norton & Co., 1978.

Rose, Rachel. "American Pageant," *Notes on Arrival and Departure*. Random House, 2005.

Rossetti, Christina. "Up-Hill," 1861.

Salah, Trish. "notes towards dropping out," *Wanting in Arabic*. TSAR, 2002.

Shaughnessy, Brenda. "I'm Over the Moon," *Human Dark with Sugar*. Copper Canyon Press, 2008.

Stein, Gertrude. "Chicken," *Tender Buttons*. 1914.

PHOTO: Bell Ancell

AMBER DAWN

is a writer, filmmaker, and performance artist, and the author
of the Lambda Award-winning novel *Sub Rosa* and the memoir *How
Poetry Saved My Life* (winner of the Vancouver Book Award). She
is also editor of *Fist of the Spider Woman: Tales of Fear and Queer
Desire* and co-editor of *With a Rough Tongue: Femmes Write Porn.*
She has an MFA in Creative Writing (UBC), and her award-winning
docuporn *Girl on Girl* has been screened in eight countries. Until
2012, she was director of programming for the Vancouver Queer
Film Festival. Amber Dawn was 2012 winner of the Writers' Trust
of Canada Dayne Ogilvie Prize for LGBT writers.

amberdawnwrites.com